28 Powerful Home Security Solutions

How to Stop Burglars from Targeting Your Home and Stealing Your Valuables

by Damian Brindle

===> Get dozens of free survival guides, hundreds of videos, 600+ "how to" articles, gear reviews and so much more here: https://rethinksurvival.com

D1526880

Disclaimer

Table of Contents

Introduction (Notes to Readers, Plus Free Stuff)

This book is intended to provide useful, actionable strategies as quickly as possible. As such, it's written to be fast to read and includes minimal images so that it remains small to download.

About Website Links

Realize, too, that this was originally written to be an electronic book only with many website links referenced throughout. Because this is a paperback book, however, referencing these links can be tedious if you had to type them into your web browser by hand. To make this easier on you, I have consolidated all referenced links into one page here: https://rethinksurvival.com/books/home-security-links.html.

When new links are introduced they will be referenced as [Link 1], [Link 2], [Link 3] and so on which will then correspond to the appropriate URL on the above referenced website page.

For completeness, however, all referenced links will also be included in Appendix B.

Grab Your Free 28-Point Checklist

Odds are that you won't remember everything discussed when you're done reading this book. To make your life easier I've created a free, easy-to-reference 28-point home security checklist which you can download that outlines everything discussed herein. You'll find a link to it here (so that you can follow along if you like) as well as at the end of this book in Appendix A, but please do read the entire book first.

Now, download your free, easy-to-reference home security checklist here: [Link 1].

Prepare Yourself for Natural Disaster in Only 5 Minutes

Since you clearly understand the need for home safety and security, I want to share with you my unique **5 Minute Survival Blueprint** where you'll discover just how to keep your family safe and secure from disasters of all kinds in only 5 minutes a day, fast, easy, and inexpensively: [Link 2].

More Survival Books You'll Enjoy

If you liked what you read when finished you can find more awesome survival books I've written at [Link 3].

This Book's Tone

As noted before, this book is written in a quick, simple, easy to read format. Hence, it is presented in a "Conversational" form and not one that is intended to be grammatically correct. Getting YOU and your family ready for emergencies is the sole focus of this book.

And My Thanks...

I also want to thank those folks who took the time to review this book, to offer their own suggestions, and to correct my mistakes... you know who you are.

Home Burglary is More Common Than You Realize

Did you know that more than 5,000 home burglaries are committed each day here in America? That's about 2,000,000 per year! I'll bet that you have been or know somebody who has been victimized in the past. Odds are you could be targeted in the future. You simply must be vigilant. Fortunately, there's plenty you can do to stop burglars from targeting you and your possessions and, equally important, to gain the upper hand in this never-ending battle.

Realize, too, that no matter how hard we try and regardless of what the statistics say, there's no way to 100% ensure that your home won't be targeted and possibly robbed. We can, however, employ many strategies to both dissuade would-be thieves and to thwart their efforts if they do choose your home. Doing so will drastically sway the odds in your favor to be sure.

This book, therefore, has been broken down into three distinct sections:

Part 1: Know Thy Enemy. Here we get to know who these people are, how they plan their heists, what factors deter their interest in your home, how (and when) they gain entry, what they're looking for once inside, as well as other considerations that may make your home more of a target than not.

Part 2: Actions to Take. Here's where we really get at the "what you can do to thwart them" ideas, specifically smart daily actions you should take, security measures to consider, why your home's first impressions really do matter, and we even tackle vacation do's and don'ts.

Part 3: 12 Secret Hiding Spots. If all your efforts have failed and they do target your home and, worse, manage to get inside then these recommendations will make their search for your valuables that much more difficult.

How to Stop Burglars, Part One: Know Thy Enemy

Getting to Know Your Adversary

To understand how to stop burglars from targeting you and your possessions we must first understand who they are and, more importantly, what their aim is. No doubt this may seem obvious since they're criminals who intend to steal whatever they can from us, but let's delve a bit deeper than that because there's a bit more to it...

First, realize that most home burglars are seasoned veterans, if you will. They know what they're doing and they know who to target. As such, **your primary defense is to make your home and valuables look less appealing than somebody else**, plain and simple.

Second, only a small portion of thieves are ever involved in other serious crimes (like assault or murder) as most of them tend to stick with burglary as their crime of choice. And, believe it or not, **most of these professional burglars are NEVER caught**... in fact, only about one in seven are ever arrested in their "career" for burglary! Again, they know what they're doing.

Third, by and large a burglar's biggest reason for stealing from you is to acquire either drugs directly (like prescription pills) or money, often to support a drug habit. Other reasons include money for partying, to buy clothes, for gambling and, oddly enough, to pay their own living expenses.

Besides cash and any form of drugs (legal or otherwise) most criminals choose to steal jewelry and electronics—especially laptops or tablets—as well as firearms since most of these items are small enough to hall away by hand and easily unloaded on the street to other criminals who then turn around and make use of your personal information as quickly as possible, including stealing your identity and depleting your bank accounts.

FYI, you can discover how to stop identity theft in my book, *Your Identity Theft Protection Game Plan*, here: [Link 4].

Planning the Heist

Most burglars rely on a vehicle, often their own, but not always. Some drive long distances—even crossing state lines—to commit the crime, though many do not. Odds are, however, that it's not the neighborhood troublemaker stealing from you... it's probably somebody who lives within a short drive of, let's say, thirty minutes and sometimes even somebody you know. Regardless, I'd keep an eye out on the neighborhood troublemaker if you've got one.

A small fraction of burglars plan their heist in advance with most of these burglaries taking place within a few days of having formulated a plan. Fortunately for home owners, these types of robberies seem to target commercial buildings, not private residences.

Most home robberies, on the other hand, are of the "spur of the moment" type and it is precisely their impulsiveness which is the reason why we can stop them from targeting you. That is, **the simple fact of making YOUR home look less appealing than somebody else will often cause them to move on**.

Last, burglars might work alone, in a team, or may even vary their tactics from time to time. I'm guessing that teams are more likely to rob commercial establishments and loners are more likely to rob homes, but that's just a guess on my part as there was no hard statistics to back this claim.

What Factors Deter Burglars?

This is where you should really start to pay attention. The first major consideration for most burglars, it seems, is general activity in and around your home, including whether you or even a dog is home. (Note: some thieves will still attempt a burglary even if you are home but, fortunately, most won't.) Beyond that, they'll want to know if there are busy streets within view of your home, if your neighbors are home and constantly peeking out of their windows, and if there are people out walking their dogs who might see them... that sort of thing.

Next, burglars will want to know if there are accessible escape routes, such as major roadways or highways nearby assuming, of course, that they're using a vehicle to make their escape. The major exception to this rule of escape route accessibility seems to be homes which are more secluded (including homes on cul-de-sacs) since there are likely to be fewer potential witnesses to the crime.

Increased security measures are, however, a huge concern for criminals. This includes alarm systems (even alarm decals to a lesser extent) and outdoor surveillance cameras. A point of note: **these MUST be real and functioning systems and not fake alarms or decals or non-functioning cameras**. Seasoned criminals can tell the difference!

The good news is that most criminals WILL be deterred by the presence of an alarm system and that most will attempt to determine if an alarm system is present beforehand; in fact, about half will stop their attempted burglary if, after gaining entry, they learn of an alarm system.

Of course, this also means that the other half will continue to ransack your home since most neighbors willfully ignore the alarm for at least a few minutes and the police often take much longer to respond, if they even will.

Gaining Entry: How, When, And What They Do After

Most burglars gain entry through open side or back doors or windows, though, some force their way through locked doors and windows while a small fraction gain entry by picking locks or by using a key they acquired previously. If they forced entry it was with small tools, such as a screwdriver, crowbar, or hammer that they brought with them. Moreover, a small fraction of burglars will cut alarm wires or telephone lines (to thwart alarm systems alerting the authorities) but this is rare.

Most home burglaries occurred during a weekday and in broad daylight while people were expected to be away at work or school... and not just you being away from home, your neighbors too. Most burglars, as I stated earlier, avoided homes when people were present, but not always. Some burglars will, horrifyingly enough, choose to rob you while you're still at home! If they choose to strike during the dark of night, however, poor lighting was a major consideration for concealing their presence and for targeting a home.

Realize that most burglars are in and out in mere minutes. They don't take long because they know where to go to get what they want... bedroom drawers and end tables, under the mattress, bedroom closets, medicine chests, and dining room drawers are the most popular poor hiding spots. Assuming you keep your valuables (e.g., money, jewelry, medicines) in any of these locations then please reconsider.

Last, evidence suggests they'll avoid going anywhere they might get trapped, such as basements or attics. Obviously, this makes accessibility of your possession by you problematic in some cases, but it's still an option to be considered.

Additional Considerations That Make You a Target

There are some other interesting points to consider, some of which you may not be able to do anything about, though you should still be aware of them:

- **Living near common offenders.** Unfortunately, some areas are more prone to crime than others and if you live near offenders then you're more likely to be robbed. While you can't do much about this fact—besides eventually moving to a "safer" area—you can, however, utilize tools to be aware of the crimes that are being reported. Sites like CrimeReports.com [Link 5] is a good one.

- **Being previously burglarized**. You might wrongly believe that if you've been burglarized in the past that, well, "lighting can't strike twice" but it can. In fact, if one thief found your house tempting then others might as well.

- **Easy hiding spots around your home's perimeter**. Thieves don't like to be seen and the more hiding spots there are the better... for them. This includes privacy fences, bushes near windows, the design of your home providing blind spots, and so on. While you cannot change the design of your home you can, for example, trim bushes and tree limbs to limit these potential hiding spots.

- **Homes with curb appeal, but not too much**. If you keep your home in good repair and live in a relatively well-off neighborhood then it is assumed there is more of a payoff to stealing from you. Homes in obvious disrepair may be ignored due to assuming there's nothing of value inside, whereas homes in very wealthy neighborhoods may also be bypassed due to the assumption of alarm systems or other security measures.

- **Acquaintances may be waiting to steal from you**. It may be your gardener, your nail lady, the auto mechanic, a neighbor, or even the delivery guy whom you just happened to mention that you're going to the Bahamas next week, who knows, but the more "loose-lipped" you are about your plans to be away from home (even on social networking sites) the more heads-up you're giving to opportunistic thieves. Granted, these folks probably aren't the seasoned vets we've been concerned with thus far, but they're no less of a concern if you give them reason and opportunity to steal from you.

Ultimately, to deter burglars, your goal is to make your home look unappealing or, put another way, "too much work" to steal from. We'll discuss how to do so in a variety of ways next, so let's get to it...

How to Stop Burglars, Part Two: 25 Vital Actions to Take

Following is a list of various actions you should consider to thwart burglars if they do take a momentary interest in your home. And, while not an exhaustive list, these are among the top actions you can and should take to make criminals pause and, more importantly, to move on...

Routines Make a Difference

1. Always shut and lock doors and windows.

Do you lock your doors whenever you leave? Do you REALLY? I know people who still don't lock their doors regularly and I'll bet you do too. In fact, according to this website [Link 6], "63% of surveyed Americans said they know people who don't lock their house doors regularly," and that, "30% of all burglaries occur with the offender entering through an unlocked door." I'd say that's a clear indication we can do better, maybe you can too.

As such, all doors and windows should be locked as often as possible when you're home, and definitely when you leave, even for short periods of time. This is especially true for ground floor doors and windows which would be the easiest access points, but don't ignore second floor or basement entryways either.

There's no reason to make a burglar's efforts any easier because they may well climb trees and second-floor decks to check. Remember, they're counting on you being lazy and choosing not to latch that too-tiny-to-climb-through bathroom window!

This advice goes for garage doors and tool sheds as well since burglars may purposefully make use of your own equipment (e.g., hand tools and ladders) to gain entry. And since such tools are usually kept in the garage or a shed, these locations are prime targets for opportunistic thieves. Keep them locked up too.

Side note: I'm part of an online neighborhood community (powered by Nextdoor.com [Link 7]) and I've seen a few instances where people said, "I just went across the street for a few minutes, so I didn't lock my door..." and it turned out somebody robbed them. Criminals really are THAT fast and they may be watching YOU, waiting for their opportunity to strike. Be vigilant no matter how fast you think you'll be, especially if you live near any heavily-trafficked location, such as a neighborhood park.

Granted, people don't always remember to lock their doors or maybe they forget to take a key with them at times. Personally, I've managed to train my family rather well over the years, so much so, that they occasionally lock me out of the house when I briefly go to the garage (it's a detached structure) only to return and find that I'm locked out. Sure, I'm not happy as I bang on the door to get somebody to open it, but I am glad they're super vigilant. Maybe one day they'll wonder where I went?

Anyway, a better option than years of training your family is to install a keypad deadbolt which can be opened and locked without a key. Fortunately, they're not terribly expensive either. Here's a good example: [Link 8].

There's more to know about your door security. Even if you lock your doors and secure the deadbolt, it's really not that hard to kick the door in as many videos, such as this one [Link 9], show. That same video also shows how a few simple changes, including replacing the small strike plate and door hinge screws with three-inch long screws, can dramatically increase the kick-in resistance of your doors. The reason why this simple fix is so useful is because the screws that were previously only held in place by the door frame are now contacting the studs which are much stronger. For only a few dollars you can buy enough screws to do every exterior door in your home. So long as your doors are relatively sturdy as the video shows, you're in good shape with this simple fix.

Fortunately, there's even more that you can do to better secure your doors, specifically by purchasing a long-throw door deadbolt, hardened strike plate, door jamb shield, or a complete door reinforcement kit, like this one: [Link 10].

2. Keep drapes and blinds closed when not at home as well.

There's no reason to let criminals know you have a 70" 4K HD television or a new, shiny laptop to steal simply by peering inside your home, especially when window drapes and blinds can be closed quickly and easily. This advice also goes for sliding glass doors, glass French doors, side window panes, small basement windows, and so on. Anything that can be peered through is fair game and should be properly obscured.

Now's the time to go through your house and start to decide which doors and windows may be looked through and, equally important, what might be visible. If necessary, wander around the outside of your home and look. What can you see through each door or window? If it's only a few family photos and a coat rack, you may be fine leaving those items visible, but if you can see your television, computers, and Louis Vuitton purse sitting on the table... cover those windows or glass doors up.

Of course, blinds or drapes may not work well in some situations, such as door glass panes or side window panes. In this case, there's some good window tint that will work almost as well as blinds, but with the obvious drawback that you won't be able to let in sunlight when desired.

That said, there are many options available, from light tint to very dark tint, "one way" film, and more; most tint is reasonably priced. I've installed window tint on relatively small windows in the past and it's not terribly difficult to do, but if you're working on very large glass panes then you may want to hire somebody to do it right. Here's an example of what I'm talking about: [Link 11].

And if that doesn't work for you then some decorative window film works great as well. We have a few doors like that and it certainly looks better than plain window tint:

3. Use appliance timers to turn lights or a radio on
   when you're not home.

You're probably aware that appliance timers are great
for vacation use, but did you know that they could be
ideal for daily use too? In fact, there are some very
sophisticated, yet relatively inexpensive, digital

appliance timers which can do more than just turn on lights at a set time each day, including varying schedules by day as well as random schedules too. Here's an example: [Link 12].

Of course, you could just leave one or two lights on and/or the radio playing at a reasonable level when you leave for the day. Doing so could be just enough to make a burglar mistakenly believe somebody is home, at least, during a cursory inspection.

Lights are clearly the best choice to leave on at night. This could be a good reason to leave the blinds or drapes open in an upstairs room, for example, though I would still close blinds or drapes on ground floor windows. (Note: To save money over time consider installing LED lights—or even the "energy saving" lights—wherever you intend to leave the lights on.)

A radio, therefore, would be the best choice as a daytime deterrence, at least, over leaving the lights on. If you don't have a radio, then a small television may suffice for this purpose. I should also point out that there are "fake televisions" which mimic the light output from a television, such as this one: [Link 13]. Personally, I'm not sold on how well they work, but they do seem to get good reviews, consume less power than a television, and may be just enough to get a thief to move on from your home.

4. If you still have a home phone, silence it while you're away.

Another trick criminals use is to get your home phone number and call it while waiting to hear the ring. After a few attempts and no answer, it's safe for them to assume that you're not home. If you silence (or otherwise muffle) the phone such that ringing cannot be heard from outside, then this will help to deter such tactics.

A similar tactic I've heard they use is to pose as some sort of local utility worker, such as those who work on water or electrical lines, or even tree services employees. They may feign an emergency or, more likely, indicate a problem they need to "check on" and would like to know "when you might be home" for them to do so. When you indicate you're "at work" or wherever, that's the green light for them to break in because they know they have at least several minutes to work with which is typically all they need. This scam, in particular, focuses on the elderly and is usually a face-to-face encounter rather than being done by phone, but people have been scammed via phone calls too.

You might be wondering by now, how easy is it to get your phone number? Rather easy, in fact. For example, a criminal can go to sites like intelius.com [Link 14] and run a quick search using a previously stolen credit card. All they need is a last name, city, and state. Surely a thief knows your city and state, and to get your last name all they need to do is to take a quick peek in your mailbox. Sadly, they can probably do all of this in a few minutes from a stolen phone or burner phone while hiding in your bushes.

Of course, if you don't have a home phone then this threat is not a problem and so long as you don't fall for the utility worker scam if they call your mobile phone, you should be safe from that one too. My advice would be to ditch the home phone if you still have one... you'll probably save money, reduce unsolicited telemarketing calls, and maybe, just maybe, stop your house form being burglarized by this scam.

5.   Park in the driveway.

I've seen it suggested that if you have a garage then you should use it to park your car since criminals may be more able to determine if you're home or not simply by watching for vehicles coming and going in the driveway.

Personally, I disagree with this strategy because, if criminals are watching you closely enough (and for long enough) to know if you're home simply by looking for cars in the driveway, then it won't matter much if you park in the garage or not because they're watching for that too.

If, on the other hand, a "spur of the moment" burglar is eyeing your house, a car or two parked in the driveway may be just enough to keep them moving along to another target. And if you happen to have an extra car that is rarely used then I would suggest parking it permanently in the driveway for this very reason.

6. Do not keep a garage door opener in your car or, at least, keep it out of view.

If you tend to park outside and you have an attached garage, then please don't keep your garage door opener in plain sight. Thieves know that many people do not lock their garage personal entry doors and thus a garage door opener offers an easy way inside your home.

Also, be sure to lock your car doors if you do park in the driveway (I know people who don't do this as well) and, if you do park inside the garage then be sure to close it after you've pulled in because, believe it or not, a thief may be brazen enough to walk into your garage and steal the garage door opener from your car, as well as anything else that may be of value inside.

No doubt, garage door openers offer easy access to at least something you value, and I'd hate to see a thief have such easy access to your belongings simply because you didn't lock your car doors when the garage door opener was clearly visible. Hide it or take the opener with you when you go inside, I do.

7. Tidy up anything a thief can use to access upper floor windows or doors.

Previously we talked about ensuring all upper-floor doors and windows are locked, and that window blinds and curtains are drawn daily. While these are good routines to follow, there's no reason to make it any easier for a burglar to gain access to upper-floor entryways either, which means we need to tidy up around the house as much as possible.

This includes putting away anything they may be able to climb onto, such as ladders. My neighbor, for instance, has kept a ladder leaning up against his back shed for years and I'm positive he has never thought twice about taking it down. Why does he keep it there and not put it up? I haven't a clue. What I do know is that if he had second-floor doors or windows (which he doesn't) that it could be used to gain access rather easily.

Unfortunately, there are some items that we can't do much about, including patio furniture, a fence next to your house, nearby trees and big tree branches, a free-standing shed, and so on. Clearly, these potential vulnerabilities can't be moved or put up as easily as a ladder. That said, it is possible to trim tree branches to make them less useful for climbing and to move patio furniture away from upper-floor entryways.

At the very least, look around your property and consider what items may be used by an opportunistic burglar to gain access to upper-floor doors or windows if you have them. There may not be much that you can do here, as noted previously, but you may find a few items to tidy up.

Additional Security Measures Not to Ignore

8. Never hide a spare key on your property, if possible, and certainly not under the doormat.

This article [Link 15] states that the top five worst places to hide a spare key include: under the doormat, a flower pot near the door, under a fake rock that clearly looks out of place, the mailbox, and really anywhere within fifteen feet of a door that the key opens.

Thieves know most people are in a hurry and don't want to work very hard to retrieve a spare key. If you must keep a key on your property, then find a not-so-obvious place well away from any doors and make sure it's relatively inaccessible. We happen to bury our key in a sprinkler head hide-a-key, such as this: [Link 16]. Again, it's not just posing as a sprinkler head, it's literally buried in a spot well away from our doors; the sprinkler head hide-a-key is merely to keep water out. In fact, see if you can spot our hidden key:

Give up yet? It's buried somewhere in that photo, which I'm positive no burglar is going to take the time to look for, but it works for us. Here it is (further buried where only the family knows the location):

Another option would be a key lock box, such as this one: [Link 17]. I know people who use this and prefer it over our strategy but be aware that by using a lock box you're betting a criminal won't be able to break into it which may or may not be the case. Alternatively, the keypad deadbolt mentioned previously would make having a spare key arguably pointless.

The best bet, however, is to give a spare key to a trusted neighbor so that they can let you in should you ever get locked out. This, of course, assumes that they'll be home to do so which may not be the case. Better yet, ask them if you may keep a spare key on their property (and they on yours) so that if a burglar did find a hidden key then it won't work for your doors and vice-versa. It's likely the sneakiest of ways to hide a spare key.

9. Don't post your name on your mailbox or other outside signage.

Surprisingly, people still happily post their last names on their mailbox, house, or other signage. I happen to have several neighbors who do this, and they don't seem to be concerned at all. Remember, however, that with a brief online name search and phone call, a thief could be done robing your house before you're finished reading this book. Keep your name off everything outside.

10. Install a wide-angle peephole.

In rare cases thieves will knock or ring the doorbell and step to the side out of view, then wait for you to answer the door and barge their way inside. How terrifying! A wide-angle peephole, while not perfect, may help you see that person hiding just out of view.

Most of the time these are easy to install (here's a tutorial showing how [Link 18]), needing only a hole of proper diameter drilled in the door. I've installed a few of these and had it finished in only a few minutes. The only caution I would suggest is that you be careful not to get too close to any door window glass when drilling the hole.

Interestingly, people are now opting for door "peephole" cameras which often allow you to record people as they come to your front door, such as this one: [Link 19]. I've yet to give one a shot myself as many such peephole cameras clearly look different than your typical peephole, which may be a good thing as it sends a clear, upfront message to would-be criminals that you're vigilant and, more importantly, that they're being recorded.

Please do some research before purchasing a peephole camera as I've noticed that some require wires to be run directly from the peephole camera to a DVR box (which is less than ideal), while others may require connection to smartphone in order to record which is also problematic since it won't be able to record activity when you're not home.

11. All non-traditional exterior doors should have secondary locking devices.

In my opinion, every exterior door should have a secondary locking device; however, this is particularly true for doors that lack deadbolts, including sliding glass doors and French doors since both designs tend to be even less secure than your typical exterior door deadbolt.

Really, any door that doesn't have a solid deadbolt (with longer strike plate and hinge screws) should be further secured with something like a door security bar, door swing bar (not a chain), or something similar. Here's the sliding doors bars which clearly indicate that you take your security seriously: [Link 20].

No doubt there are other ways to better secure exterior sliding doors, some of which cost little to no money. For instance, you could simply cut a piece of 1"x2" and lay that in the track of a sliding door rather than buying a security bar. Personally, I like the security bar because it's clearly visible from outside and clearly indicates you take your security seriously.

In addition, you could also drill a hole in the sliding glass door and door frame and insert a small nail to prevent the door from being lifted. (FYI, there are inexpensive solutions meant for this purpose: [Link

21].) Whatever you choose to use, you just need to be careful not to contact the door glass when drilling the hole. If you're not comfortable doing so, then hire somebody.

Also, these door swing bar locks (they come in different finishes) are good for most exterior swing-open doors as an added level of security: [Link 22]. We have them on almost every exterior door and keep them latched whenever possible:

French-style doors are also a problem because one door is expected to act as the securing point for the other door; this is usually accomplished with two sliding latches at the top and bottom of the stationary door. While better than nothing, these sliding latches aren't very secure either. To help prevent these doors from being kicked in, use a door brace: [Link 23].

Personally, I use one of these for a door that doesn't have a deadbolt, as shown here:

Granted, even a door brace won't help French doors if they're mostly glass. A neat option to tackle this problem would be window security film: [Link 24]. It's similar to the window tint mentioned earlier, but resists breakage and keeps glass shards together when broken thereby making the glass much more difficult to break through. While it is an expensive option, window security film is about the best we can do for securing door and window glass from breakage, that is, without either replacing the door or glass.

Side note: I should point out that pet doors (you can see we had one in the above photo) should be boarded up if no longer needed or have a secondary latch added to that door.

Finally, all other structures on your property that have doors should have locks, including detached garages, sheds, and even fence gates. There's no reason to make access to anything on your property easy for a thief.

12. Windows should have additional locks as well.

While doors are the obvious security threat, windows cannot be ignored as they may be an even easier entry point than most doors. And because most homes have many more windows than doors, you really need to pay special attention to them.

Clearly there are many types of window designs, but most either slide open horizontally or vertically, or they swing open outwardly. Each window needs a different solution.

To better secure windows that slide open horizontally, a simple dowel rod or small piece of wood inserted in the window track will help, just like with the sliding glass doors. We happen to have a bunch of windows like this and so I cut several pieces of wood to fit them as shown here:

Unfortunately, some older windows can be lifted from their track. To prevent this, it's possible to insert a locking pin, again, just like the sliding glass doors.

And, though I've never tried it, I've heard you can glue something like a #2 pencil to the upper window track such that when the window is in the closed position the pencil rests between the window and the track thereby filling the gap which previously allowed the window to be lifted. You will, of course, need to experiment with this idea before making use of it.

For vertical windows, you can do something similar to the wooden dowel idea or buy real window security bars, such as these: [Link 25], which also happen to work for horizontal sliding windows. There are other styles of windows locks, if you prefer, but I'm partial to security bars because they're sturdier and, again, clearly show you take your security seriously.

Swing-open windows (also known as casement windows) are fairly secure so long as you close and lock them. I should point out that some windows swing open inwardly and may be easily bypassed as a result. Watch this video [Link 26] for how to prevent that problem.

Ultimately, you need to look at each of your windows and decide how a criminal may be able to bypass their traditional locking mechanisms because, trust me, they know how.

13. Remove the end from your garage door pull release handle.

Did you know that thieves may be able to use the garage door release handle to open your garage door from the outside even when closed? It's like how the tow truck guy can shim and unlock your car door with a coat hanger of sorts in only a few minutes. Here's a video showing how easy it is to break-in this way [Link 27].

Basically, you'll want to remove the pull handle from the garage door release cord so that it's not available for a thief to make use of in this fashion:

REMOVE PULL HANDLE

To fully ensure that a thief cannot gain access to your garage in this fashion, use a small zip tie to keep the actual release lever from being easily moved:

Just be aware that it will take a bit more force to break the zip tie when pulling the handle and that a larger zip tie will require more force; too large of a zip tie and it may not break without a lot of effort and potential damage to your garage door rail or related parts. Personally, I've found that a small four-inch zip tie worked out well and could be broken easily enough when pulling down on the cord.

If you choose to zip tie the lever as shown above, be sure that the zip tie won't interfere with the chain mechanism of the garage door system in any way as I would hate to see you have an expensive garage door repair because of this simple security fix.

Side note: Another possibility is that a thief can use a "code grabber" device to steal your garage door signal whenever you use your garage door opener. Apparently, however, newer garage doors don't have this vulnerability due to "rolling code" technology.

14. Get a dog.

According to a U.S. Department of Justice report [Link 28], "A dog's presence is a close substitute for human occupancy, and most burglars avoid houses with dogs. Small dogs may bark and attract attention, and large dogs may pose a physical threat, as well. On average, burglarized houses are less likely to have dogs than are non-burglarized houses, suggesting that dog ownership is a substantial deterrent."

While the above statement makes it sound like having a dog will prevent your home from being burglarized, it will not. Some thieves are undeterred by the presence of a dog in your home and will merely distract them to gain entry or, worse, physically harm them. More often, however, dogs are simply barricaded in whatever room they're confined to while the burglars ransack the rest of your home.

Though larger dog breeds are obviously more frightening, smaller dogs tend to make more noise which may attract attention and is precisely what criminals don't want. Those "beware of dog" signs are useful too but—assuming you don't have a dog— make sure there is supporting evidence of a dog on property, such as a used dog bowl on the back porch, a large leash within view, maybe dog toys or an old dog house out back, etc.

Ultimately, the presence of a dog won't prevent a burglary; however, they may be just enough to deter a thief, especially if you have nearby neighbors who may be alerted to unusual activity.

One last point: If you're interested in getting a dog for this purpose, then find out if he or she actually barks. We, for instance, happened to rescue a dog from the shelter a while back and, as it turns out, he doesn't bark because of his breeding. We didn't know that at the time and most days I'm thankful that he doesn't bark nonstop like our last dog. And, though we didn't get him for security purposes, his presence sure won't do us any good should the need ever arise.

15. Request a security inspection from local authorities.

Your local police or insurance company may offer a free service where they come into your home and assess security. Sometimes it's helpful to have another set of eyes pointing out deficiencies.

16. Join or create a neighborhood watch.

Studies have shown, at least for lower income neighborhoods, that a functioning neighborhood watch deters crime. That said, it seems the results are mixed with respect to middle- and upper-class neighborhoods. Really, the idea behind a neighborhood watch is just about neighbors looking out for neighbors. Get to know them so they get to know you and, of course, so you both get to know who doesn't belong. Finally, ensure signs are prominently posted:

First Impressions Really Do Matter

17. Trees and shrubs should be trimmed regularly.

A burglar wants as little attention drawn to them as possible. That means no noise and especially no eyeballs watching them as they case your house from the outside. Obviously, the more hiding spots there are for them to plot their break-in, the better.

Now, while you could be extreme and remove as many bushes and trees on your property as possible, most of us prefer a bit of nature to look at. As such, the next best option is to keep bushes, shrubs, and trees well-trimmed, especially next to windows and doors, though, all landscaping should be kept tidy to reduce potential hiding spots anywhere in your yard, including along fence lines.

Following is an example from my own yard. It's obvious that I have some cleanup to do here since you can't even see my neighbor's house behind this overgrowth:

In my defense, I have A LOT of yard to keep up with since I basically live in the woods here in the Pacific

Northwest. Regardless, a mess like this clearly needs trimmed up!

A tidy yard also signals to thieves that you're attentive to your home and are, therefore, less likely to leave a door unlocked or window unlatched. At least, that's an assumption I'm willing to make.

By now I hope it's clear that you really should get outside and wander around your property to see your home from a would-be burglar's perspective. What can be made use of to gain entry? Where might a burglar hide while they plot their heist? What doors or windows are easily accessible? Asking these questions will help you understand where you're vulnerable and, therefore, help you to fix them.

18. Install motion-sensing lights where possible.

Exterior lights also make a difference, especially along the driveway and near exterior doors. That said, anywhere you can light up around your home is probably a good thing to do because it offers fewer hiding spots to criminals at night. Here I have hardwired lights that cover two sides of my house and much of the driveway:

While hardwired lights are much brighter, they do make relatively decent wireless motion sensing spotlights, such as those made by Mr. Beams for areas where running electrical wires may not be easy or feasible, such as a detached shed: [Link 29]. I've got a few of these and they work well enough for this purpose, plus I don't have to replace the batteries more than once a year:

BATTERY-POWERED MOTION LIGHT ARE GREAT FOR HARD TO REACH LOCATIONS!

Also, try to install motion-sensing lights up high or where they would be hard to reach so they're not easily disabled, such as by removing the light bulb or by covering up the sensor.

Perhaps an even better option is to leave lights on full time at night. We happen to have neighbors that keep specific, rather bright, lights on all night long. And, while it bothers my wife because she prefers absolute darkness to sleep, I don't mind so much because it clearly illuminates an entire side of our house, thereby eliminating many potential hiding spots. Thanks neighbors! You'll have to decide what works best for your situation.

19. Don't leave expensive toys in plain sight.

This could be anything from a John Deere riding lawn mower to dirt bikes or your boat. These items scream "I spend money on stuff!" Keep them locked away in a shed or garage, if possible.

20. Fences are a double-edged sword.

Fences tend to say, "stay out," yet offer additional secrecy for thieves, particularly the taller six-foot privacy fences many people prefer. Here's an example (also in my own backyard) where the combination of a privacy fence and a lack of trimmed bushes can make for easy hiding spots, both on my side of the fence as well as for my neighbor:

If you already have a fence there isn't much to do except to ensure bushes are trimmed so that they don't offer much of a hiding place on your side of the fence.

If you're in the market for a fence, however, then you might think twice before adding one because, regrettably, they won't add to your home security. If you insist on having one, maybe the best option is to split the difference and have a smaller three- or four-foot fence instead of a larger six-foot one. Of course, there are many fence designs out there and, so, some research should be done before doing what everyone else does where you live.

Vacations and Holidays Are No Time to Relax, Thieves Are Hard at Work

21. Ensure somebody trustworthy grabs your mail, newspapers, and even fliers left on your front door.

Burglars are constantly on the lookout for anything which indicates people are home or not. And there's nothing like a pile of newspapers on your doorstep to tell them you haven't been home in a while, come on in!

This problem is easily fixed by having a neighbor pick up newspapers for you while you're on vacation. Of course, it's almost as easy to put a stop to your deliveries too. I would suggest doing so whenever possible.

Not surprisingly, thieves have also been known to leave advertisement fliers on the front door and then come back the next day to check if they've been grabbed as another indication of activity. It can't hurt to ask a neighbor or even to pay a neighbor kid to grab these items for you. Besides, it will be a good excuse for them to check on your property each day.

22. Mailboxes are another clue.

Just as with newspapers and fliers, your mailbox being crammed full of mail is another indication you're not home. Luckily, this is an easy one to thwart simply by purchasing a locking mailbox which, incidentally, reduces mail theft... another rising crime that leads to identity theft. If you don't yet have a locking mailbox or get way too much mail, ask a neighbor to pick it up daily or have the USPS hold your mail [Link 30].

Sadly, however, it's possible—albeit unlikely—that dishonest postal service or delivery service employees may take advantage of the knowledge that you've stopped your mail deliveries which clearly indicates you're not home as well... yet another reason to just ask a neighbor to get these items for you while you're away. Personally, I wouldn't worry too much about this particular threat, though burglaries have happened as a result of this knowledge [Link 31].

23. Park a vehicle in the driveway.

As I've mentioned before, parking in the driveway is a good strategy to deter burglars in general. During vacation, however, it's even more important because there will be fewer indications than normal that the house is occupied.

Better yet, ask your neighbor to park in your driveway. While having a vehicle in the driveway indicates people are home, a vehicle that NEVER moves might give your ruse away. A neighbor, however, who is expected to be using their car regularly and who parks in your driveway makes the ruse that much more believable.

Perhaps the best course of action, therefore, is to do both: park your own vehicle in the driveway while you're gone and ask your neighbor to use your driveway as well.

24. Request an occasional drive by from local authorities.

This may or may not help, but alerting the local police that you'll be away for an extended period and request they check on the place periodically couldn't hurt. Honestly, about the best this will do if a thief really has targeted your home is for the authorities to note the mess and board up your doors, if they'll even do that much. Maybe you'll get a phone call.

25. Holiday garbage should be slowly and carefully disposed of.

Seeing as though the holidays are a common time for people to be on vacation, you should be aware that thieves have been known to check the trash (and recycling) during the weeks following the holidays, specifically looking for boxes which indicate new and expensive purchases, such as laptops, tablets, and gaming systems. I would encourage you to take your time disposing of these boxes, to turn them inside out if able, and to cut them down as much as possible to make their contents less easily identifiable by thieves.

The Three Most Effective Security Measures, Hands-Down

1. Add a Security Alarm System

If there's ONE deterrent that stands out above all others, it's a functioning alarm system. According to various statements [Link 32], "About 60% of the burglars indicated that the presence of an alarm would cause them to seek an alternative target altogether. This was particularly true among the subset of burglars that were more likely to spend time deliberately and carefully planning a burglary." That's nothing to take lightly. If the mere presence of an alarm system would deter more than half of burglars, that's great news!

Realize that there are plenty of alarm system options out there, even relatively inexpensive DIY options, but an alarm system that is expected to alert the authorities is probably the best bet. I have family who, for example, use SimpliSafe.com [Link 33] and absolutely love it. There are clearly other choices out there and plenty of advice as to which is best. Personally, I doubt it matters too much which alarm system you choose, so long as you use it every day like you're supposed to which, unbelievably, many people do not.

That said, police response time to home alarms is often abysmal and thieves know that too. Coupled with the fact that most neighbors will ignore a blaring alarm siren for several minutes, thieves may blatantly ignore your alarm for these very reasons and choose to rob you anyway. Consequently, an alarm shouldn't be considered the be-all and end-all solution.

It is, however, about the best we can do as a deterrent for stopping a burglar from considering your home further, and even to stop them in the act after they've gained entry. Be sure to prominently display any window decals or signage (including on side windows or back doors) so that thieves are quickly alerted to your alarm system.

If you can't afford a real alarm system then the next potential option may be to purchase alarm system decals, though, it appears that most thieves can tell the difference. Yes, this isn't nearly as good of an option, but it may be just enough to thwart a few criminals... the lazy ones, anyway. Last, alarms systems often reduce insurance rates. Check with your insurance company to be sure and to get specifics.

2. Add Surveillance Equipment

If a quality alarm system is the number one way to thwart criminals, working cameras are the second-best way to do so. In fact, I found a few articles which stated [Link 34] that, "the most effective deterrents for home burglaries and car theft were CCTV [closed circuit television] cameras…" according to those burglars interviewed, but that information seemed to stem from the United Kingdom. Regardless, cameras are always touted as one of the two best ways to deter crime.

The question, therefore, is: where and how many? That is, should they be placed inside the home or outside? And how many will you need?

The answer to the first question, inside or out, is easy: do both if you can afford it, but since we're talking about home burglaries then it makes sense to have cameras inside to catch them in the act. There are, however, two major problems with this choice: (1) homeowners are reluctant to place cameras inside bedrooms for privacy concerns even though bedrooms are the most likely rooms to be targeted, and (2) cameras inside the home do nothing to deter burglars from choosing to rob you in the first place.

If, on the other hand, cameras are clearly visible outside on the outside, then it makes sense that they will act as a strong deterrent to burglarizing your home even before gaining entry which, after all, is what we're trying to accomplish here. Therefore, if you had to choose between inside or out, choose outside cameras.

Now, the question is how many cameras will you need? This is more difficult to answer. At the very least, being able to cover all sides of your house is a start. Unfortunately, doing so isn't as easy as installing four cameras, one pointed at each side of your home, and calling it good. For example, sometimes homes have odd shapes or recesses that may need their own monitoring, a detached garage or shed may need several cameras alone, and usually a front or backyard would be nice to monitor as well. In most cases we're talking at minimum several cameras which can get rather expensive, at least, for the better systems out there.

To make matters worse, there's something to be said for having to run a bunch of wires to connect them all. And, while wireless cameras are becoming more popular and more reliable, a hard-wired system still seems to be the best bet here, particularly for reliability and image quality. Sadly, adding so many cameras can get even more expensive than adding a DIY alarm system. Regardless, there is something to be said for the peace of mind a surveillance system brings—even while you're at home—because many systems can be connected to your television and viewed at a moment's notice, even recorded for later review.

For example, I have a family member who has at least a dozen hard-wired cameras connected to a dedicated television mounted on a wall where he can easily glance at it and see all sides of his house, the yards, driveway, and front door. Plus, the feeds are constantly recorded for later review or to give to the police, if necessary. Such systems are really a great way to go if you can afford it. I'd recommend Lorex camera systems as a quality option for the price, though, there are other great choices. You can also find Lorex cameras at Costco if you have a membership and even Amazon.com as well, here's an example: [Link 35].

Combine a quality alarm system with surveillance cameras and it would take an extremely motivated—and probably not very smart— thief to choose your home as a target.

3. Prepare for Your Most Valuable Possessions to be Stolen

I know this advice feels counterintuitive, but no matter how vigilant we are or even if we've done everything in our power to thwart break-in's, sometimes the bad guys still win and manage to steal what's ours. To recover from the ordeal as quickly as possible—and to minimize additional trouble for you in the future—there's a few more specific actions to take...

Insurance Riders (your most prized possession may not be covered without them)

Let's talk about insurance first. Many of us mistakenly believe that if, heaven-forbid, our expensive possessions were ever stolen that homeowner's insurance will cover the loss and, at the very least, replace what's been taken. This may or may not be true.

You see, some rather expensive items, such as jewelry, may exceed your homeowner's insurance coverage or, depending upon your insurer, may not be covered at all. You need to ask about insurance riders, also known as an "endorsements" or "scheduled personal property" to ensure you're fully covered. Which of your personal possessions likely need an insurance rider? There are several, including:

- Jewelry (e.g., an expensive watch, ring, or necklace)
- Fine art / artwork (e.g., paintings, sculptures)
- Antiques (e.g., oriental rugs, heirloom furniture)
- Dining/drinking sets (e.g., fine china, sterling silverware, crystal glasses)
- Electronics / home office equipment (computers, scanners, cameras, laptops)
- Collectibles (e.g., autographs, stamps, comic books, musical instruments)

- Firearms (especially collectibles)

Basically, if your possessions go beyond the typical television, couch, and bedroom furniture, ask your insurance provider about riders because the odds are that you'll need one. Here's more information about hidden valuables [Link 36] in your home so you have a better idea of what to ask about.

Firearms (you may be legally responsible to report theft)

While it appears that you shouldn't typically be held criminally liable for crimes committed with your stolen firearms, you're still going to want to report theft to the authorities as soon as possible for several reasons, though mainly to return your firearm to you should they ever be recovered.

In fact, reporting theft of your firearms may be state law, as explained here [Link 37]: "Laws that require firearm owners to notify law enforcement about the loss or theft of a firearm serve several public safety functions. These laws help deter gun trafficking and straw purchasing, and help law enforcement recover and return lost or stolen guns to their rightful owners. They also help law enforcement disarm individuals who become ineligible to possess firearms."

By and large, the most important piece of information to report to the authorities is the firearm's serial number, although it couldn't hurt to include additional identifying information, such as make, model, date and location of purchase, any unique identifying marks, and so on. Therefore, be sure to record each firearm's serial number and keep that information in a secure place, such as a fire safe.

Report theft to the local authorities, ensuring they clearly understand that a firearm has been stolen (especially if many items have been stolen) as well as to the BATFE (Bureau of Alcohol, Tobacco, Firearms and Explosives) via their Stolen Firearms Hotline number at 888-930-9275. You'll also want to alert your insurance company; whether to file a claim is up to you.

Handheld Electronics (and the goldmine they contain)

Now, while items like cash, jewelry, and firearms are prime targets for thieves, as mentioned previously, so are small electronics, especially laptops, tablets, and smartphones. This isn't to say that entire computers couldn't be targeted, it's just that handheld electronics are preferred because they're easier to carry off.

Besides apparently being easy to sell on the streets, small electronics are rife with personal information that make stealing your money and identity much easier. In fact, if you ever do discover that ANY of your electronics have been stolen or lost… panic… but only for a moment because you've got work to do.

Fortunately, there are some steps that you should take now, before your electronics get stolen, to make things easier on you later or to slow down would-be identity thieves. They are:

- **Record all serial numbers** (write it down on paper or put it in the Cloud) for every handheld device you own, including laptops, tablets, and smartphones.
- **Use "Find my Device" services**. Some handheld electronics include this feature though, if you have a Google account, you can get this service for free [Link 38] no matter what type of handheld device you use. Laptops may need a different solution, such as AbsoluteLoJack.com [Link 39] or GadgetTrack.com [Link 40]—which both cost money—to potentially locate and recover not only your laptop, but handheld electronics too. Other options, such as LockItTight.com [Link 41] and PreyProject.com [Link 42] offer limited free tracking services.
- **Password-protect everything**. Every handheld device (including laptops) should have a startup password or a screen lock on them. While laptop passwords can apparently be bypassed relatively easily with software,

smartphone's may be more difficult. Regardless, don't underestimate the speed with which a thief can gain access to your electronics even if they're password-protected.

- **Be wary of wiping data**. Sometimes smartphones or tablets (especially iPhones and iPads) allow you to erase all data after ten failed login attempts. This may be a great if they're ever stolen, but horrifying if a young child ever gets hold of it!

- **Encrypt sensitive computer data instead**. A better option would be to encrypt sensitive laptop files or folders using various methods, including free software. Here's a tutorial on how to encrypt [Link 43] Windows files and folders, in particular. Personally, I would use the VeraCrypt option outlined in the link because it will encrypt files even if a criminal gains access to your user login information, though, you'll need a password to access that data each time you login to your computer.

- **Avoid accessing files and folders on smart devices, or use the Cloud**. For tablets and smartphones, either avoid keeping and accessing sensitive files on them or move data to the Cloud. Doing so minimizes offline access to such sensitive information and, at the very least, gives you a chance to change

Cloud account passwords or to deauthorize a device before any harm is done.

- **Move data to a portable USB device and backup regularly regardless**. Another option is to move sensitive files to an external USB drive and to ONLY access them on that drive. You would then move this external drive to a secure place (like a fire safe) after each time you use it. Personally, this is too much trouble for me, but if you find yourself only accessing such information infrequently, then it may be a good choice. At the very least, an external USB drive is great for doing regular backups of your files and folders; I do this regularly in the event my laptop crashes, but this practice will also help with recovery from theft.

If your electronics are ever stolen, however, you're going to want to report the theft to the police and possibly to your insurance company as well. They probably won't care much at all, but that's the right thing to do and may just help you get your electronics back if they're ever recovered.

More importantly, immediately change the passwords for all your sensitive websites, including emails and social media, and especially your financial institutions. Honestly, every website that has any personal information about you should be changed. This is going to be a nightmare and really time consuming, but you cannot ignore how important this is. Personally, we keep a printed list of all our important websites that would need to be changed (along with passwords) in a secure spot for this very reason.

Last, if you've been victimized, I would encourage you to monitor all your bank and credit card accounts very closely, your credit report, as well as email and passwords... really anything associated with your identity for many months, even years afterwards because it could take that long for your information to circulate to those willing to abuse it.

How to Stop Burglars, Part Three: 12 Sneaky Hiding Spots

Following are a dozen of my favorite methods for hiding your valuables and survival supplies. These are but a fraction of the many sneaky methods you'll uncover to hide your valuables from nosy neighbors, thieves, looters, and worse inside my book, *75 of the Best Secret Hiding Places*, found here: [Link 44].

Inside you'll discover precisely how to hide valuables in plain sight as well as how to hide your survival supplies when times get tough. Trust me when I tell you that these are "just the tip of the iceberg" of what's covered within. Click the link above and discover all 75 ways to hide your valuables. Now, here's a dozen of my favorite ideas:

1. **Commercially-made diversion safes**.

There are myriads of interesting diversion safes found online. You can find everything under the sun, from books to cans of shaving cream, soda cans, clocks, batteries, lighters, and more. Many of these look so real that YOU might get fooled yourself when trying to find the diversion safe.

Sadly, I'd suspect that many thieves know about these types of diversion safes and may, therefore, be on the lookout for them. To be honest, I don't foresee many thieves stopping to try and unscrew the bottom of a can of shaving cream he finds in my bathroom just to check, but who knows what they're willing to do if given time.

Regardless, if you're interested, just go to Amazon.com and search for "diversion safe" and you'll find a wide variety of options.

2. **Make your own diversion safe**.

If you're worried about the commercially-made diversion safes being compromised, make your own unique diversion safe instead. I did this with little more than a vegetable can and pill bottle [Link 45] and it worked out rather well, so much so that I'd happily recommend the idea.

I'll virtually guarantee that even the most determined "snatch and grab" thief isn't going to go through my cupboard looking through all my canned vegetables hoping to find a diversion safe. It's so devious that I'm willing to bet my valuables on it.

Clearly, you're not going to be able to fit a whole lot inside of a vegetable can safe, but you can certainly add a wad of cash, which brings up a good point: whatever you choose to add to these mini safes should be well insulated from a cursory inspection. For instance, don't add a bunch of gold coins to a diversion safe such that it makes a lot of noise when the can is grabbed or weighs five times as much as a normal can of green beans does.

3. **Hollowed-out books**.

I'd imagine you've seen this idea before, but it's a good one to use because most people totally ignore books. If you don't want to ruin one of your own books, then you can certainly buy very inexpensive books at a used book store or even online for only a few dollars and simply cut out a space to hide your stuff. Here's an example video [Link 46] on how to do so.

Be sure to opt for a bigger book so that you can hide more stuff; something like a medical text would be perfect. I've even seen people glue entire book volumes (hollowed out) to make larger diversion safes, but doing so will leave a larger chance of your valuables being found because a burglar must only uncover the entire volume of books rather than a single book to find your hidden stash.

4. **Move your real valuables safe away from your bedroom**.

Like I said before, burglars know we're lazy and prefer easy access to items such as a fire safe or jewelry box where we're most likely to want them, that being our bedroom or the bedroom closet. I'd suggest moving your real valuables safe as far away as possible, such as into the basement, laundry room, a kid's room, or maybe a shed or garage if whatever is inside won't get ruined by the temperature or humidity (but it probably will, so inside the house is best).

To throw them off, though, buy an inexpensive fire safe and fill it with a few goodies like costume jewelry that rattles around inside to perk their interest and keep that in your bedroom closet where it's easy for a thief to find. The expectation is that they'll choose to grab the diversion safe and never bother to look for another one. Here's a good, inexpensive safe for this purpose: [Link 47].

5. **Create a wall outlet safe**.

Honestly, if a thief is thorough enough to check your wall outlets for valuables then you're in for a long day. Assuming they're not quite that thorough then this idea is a sneaky one to be sure. Here's a video on how to convert a wall outlet into a safe [Link 48] or you can buy one, in which case you'll only have to cut out a hole in your drywall and you're done: [Link 49].

Just be sure to place this outlet in an out-of-the-way spot, such as behind the couch or a piece of furniture, and in-line with other outlets so it doesn't look suspicious.

6. **Laundry, utility, mud rooms**.

Oftentimes these rooms aren't finished or, at least, have quite a bit of potential space to hide supplies. The best part is that they'll be overlooked by most thieves because nobody is expected to keep anything of value here.

You could, for instance, consider hiding items behind the washer or dryer, high in cabinets and behind laundry supplies, or down low under sinks. Since these rooms are so different you really must look at your own situation to decide how best to use it.

The point is that they'll be overlooked by most thieves. Be aware, however, that these rooms can get both warm and moist (assuming there's a dryer present) so it might not be the best place for foodstuffs or anything that doesn't do well in humid conditions.

7. **Atop high kitchen cabinets.**

Maybe you'd prefer to go high rather than low? Instead of merely collecting dust, you can certainly hide some small valuables atop your kitchen cabinets, specifically cabinets with added crown moldings. If the cabinet molding isn't tall enough to obscure one's view you can try replacing (or adding onto) the existing molding, if this interests you.

Be sure that the view truly is obscured by looking at your now hidden stash from different angles and different distances… and if you're short, like me, then stand on a chair to check.

In addition, there's sometimes a usable gap where cabinet sections meet, in-between which you can slip an envelope of money or other important documents, for example.

8. **Inside filing cabinets**.

For some reason filing cabinets are completely uninteresting to most people, including criminals. Mark them with something boring like "2015 taxes" and they're sure never to open the drawer… unless they're identity thieves, in which case you should read my book, *Your Identity Theft Protection Game Plan*, here: [Link 50].

Regardless, it can't hurt to also lock the drawers to keep prying eyes at bay. Heck, you could even go so far as to include some actual files inside one drawer that was "accidentally" left unlocked. Just know that some filing cabinet locks are easily bypassed by a determined individual, so don't expect your valuables to be secure simply because they're behind a now locked drawer.

9. **Up high in a child's closet**.

It seems that burglars tend to bypass children's rooms never expecting to find anything of value inside. Use this to your advantage and hide your valuables there. Typically, high up on a closet shelf, shoved behind some old stuffed animals or blankets works great.

The only caveat I would argue is if you have a teenager. Their rooms might be considered slightly more interesting because they could have more valuable items to steal, such as gaming consoles, cash, clothing, and so on. Young children's rooms, on the other hand, are probably a safer hiding spot.

10. **Inside the freezer**.

Wrap your valuables inside a few layers of aluminum foil, then inside a plastic freezer bag or two, mark it "hamburger" or something like that, and nobody's the wiser. Hidden inside a bag of flour or container of yeast or any other ubiquitous foodstuff would work just as well too.

11. **Paint cans and buckets**.

Old cans of empty, dried out paint—when stashed with other cans of paint—are a great place that few will ever think to look. I've even heard of people going so far as to hide actual valuables inside large buckets of nearly full paint. Now THAT is dedication! Regardless, odds are that you have several cans of paint lying around and that one of them may be useful for this purpose.

And, just as with the cat litter and trash can ideas, you really do want to minimize odors from paint. Of course, another thought would be to purchase a new, unused paint can. The only problem is that it may stand out next to the clearly used cans of paint. With a little effort, however, you could make this new paint can look used by smearing paint around the outside and the lid, maybe slapping a label on the lid and side... that sort of thing.

I also want to mention buckets here. I don't know about you, but I've got a lot of larger five- and six-gallon "homer" buckets lying around my garage for a variety of reasons. Clearly, these buckets can hold quite a bit and may very well be overlooked, especially if they're grungy or labeled innocuously.

12. **In-wall safes**.

There are a wide variety of in-wall safes available for purchase. In fact, there are both obvious ones and even hidden safes, such as those depicted in this mirror safe video [Link 51]. Although the idea is to store firearms inside, you can really store anything you like if it fits.

The question, of course, is where to put your safe. By now I hope you realize that your bedroom is a poor choice. Granted, odds are that even if a thief were to find your hidden wall safe that they either wouldn't be able to access it, or they wouldn't be able to completely remove it to work on opening later.

No matter where you choose to install your hidden wall safe, at least place it behind something like a painting or mirror so that it's not readily obvious. And, as always, the more difficult it is for you to access the more difficult it will be for a thief.

Home Security Recap

Thieves are fast and smarter than most folks give them credit for. They're in and out in minutes and want easy to grab items, such as cash, jewelry, firearms, and medications, as well as small electronics, especially laptops and tablets. Do your best to hide or secure these items.

Remember that your primary goal is to get thieves to decide your home is too much effort and that they should just move on to an easier target. You need to be both vigilant and diligent...

Keep up with your security routines by locking doors and windows when you leave, ensuring drapes and blinds are shut as often as possible, and making it look like your home is occupied by turning on lights, radios, or televisions while you're gone. A dog's presence helps too, though they aren't assured deterrents whatsoever.

Increase door and window security with secondary locks, particularly if you have easily thwarted entryways, such as sliding glass doors, French doors, or old, sliding windows. Of course, don't ignore upper-floor windows or doors because burglars will specifically target them no matter how difficult you think they are to access from the outside.

Take away those outside hiding spots too. Specifically, ensure your yard is kept up, trees and bushes are trimmed, and fence lines cleared too. Install exterior lights, including motion-sensing lights to reduce hiding spots at night while you're at it; cover the obvious entrances, but light up as much as possible if you're able to do so.

Avoid being lazy, that is, don't hide an easily accessible spare key on your property, don't leave your garage door opener in your car, and try not to leave expensive "toys" outside (e.g., motorcycles, riding lawnmowers, etc.) that indicate you have a lot of goodies inside to steal.

Remember, too, that vacations and holidays are no time to relax. Ensure your mail and newspapers are picked up or deliveries stopped, and park a vehicle in the driveway when you're gone for any length of time. Additionally, after the holidays garbage should be slowly and carefully disposed of because you never know who's paying attention.

Ultimately, the addition of an alarm system and/or exterior security camera setup are the most useful deterrents to would-be thieves. Studies show repeatedly that these are your best bets. Just ensure they work properly, cover all doors and windows, and that they're used regularly.

Finally, be prepared for your most valuable of possessions to be stolen. Get insurance riders, report theft of firearms and electronics immediately, and be sure to act now to protect yourself if any handheld electronics are ever stolen, including recording serial numbers, using "find my device" software, password-protecting devices, encrypting data, and so on. You won't regret taking the time now should you ever fall victim down the road.

Get Your Free 28-Point Checklist Here

Before you grab your checklist, be a good friend or family member and choose to help others who could use this crucial information...

Spread the Word, Share the Knowledge

I'm willing to bet that you have family and friends who could benefit from this book as well, so please take a moment right now and quickly share a link to it on Facebook, Twitter, or Pinterest... you can easily do so here: [Link 52].

Now, download your free, easy-to-reference home security checklist here: [Link 53].

Discover More Great Survival Books Here

If you liked what you read within then you're going to love my other survival books: [Link 54]. Here's a sampling, just click on any book title below to find out more or use the link provided above to see them all...

- ➤ 53 Essential Bug Out Bag Supplies [Link 55]
- ➤ 47 Easy DIY Survival Projects [Link 56]
- ➤ The Complete Pet Safety Action Plan [Link 57]
- ➤ 27 Crucial Smartphone Apps for Survival [Link 58]
- ➤ 37 Scientifically-Proven Survival Foods to Stockpile [Link 59]
- ➤ 75 of the Best Secret Hiding Places [Link 60]
- ➤ Your Identity Theft Protection Game Plan [Link 61]
- ➤ 144 Survival Uses for 10 Common Items [Link 62]

And if you would like to be among the first to know when new survival books become available, fill out this form and you'll be notified via email: [Link 63].

Recommended for You...

I want to point out one book from the above list, in particular, since you clear recognize the need for security and safety: *Your Identity Theft Protection Game Plan: 7 Critical Steps to Prevent the Fastest Growing Crime in America From Happening to You.*

According to the FBI, "Identity theft is one of the fastest growing crimes in the U.S., claiming more than 10 million victims a year."

Guess what? That statement was from 2004!

Worse, according to the U.S. Department of Justice more than 17 million Americans were victims of identity theft in 2014.

Obviously, identity theft is on the rise and only getting worse as we continue to move our lives to a digital existence.

You simply MUST take appropriate steps NOW to avoid long-lasting and far-reaching consequences later.

Click here to discover [Link 63b] precisely how to protect yourself, your assets, and your privacy from cybercriminals today.

Your Opinion Matters to Me

I'd love to hear your feedback about this book, especially anything I might be able to add or improve upon for future revisions. Please send me an email at rethinksurvival@gmail.com with the word "book" in the subject if you have something for me. (And be sure to include the book title so I'm not confused.)

Why You Should Review This Book...

Because reviews are critical in spreading the word about books, I ask that you take a moment and write a review of the book so that others know what to expect, particularly if you've found my advice useful: [Link 64]. (Note: you'll be sent to Amazon.com to write the review after clicking this link.)

I do hope that you've enjoyed this book and that you will choose to implement my recommendations to help keep your home and possessions safe from determined thieves.

I encourage you to please take a moment and download the checklist above, share this book with your friends and family using the link I provided previously, and leave a quick review on Amazon.com while you're at it.

May God bless you and your family. Thank you for your time, Damian

Appendices

Appendix A: 28-Point Checklist

Appendix B: List of Resources

Appendix A: 28-Point Checklist

Routines Make a Difference

1. Always shut and lock doors (including door deadbolts) and windows (especially ground floor windows but don't ignore second floor windows either) when leaving the home.
2. Keep drapes and blinds closed when not at home (no need to let them see what you have).
3. Use timers to turn on lights/radio when not home, or just leave a few lights on when you go.
4. If you still have a home phone, silence it while you're away.
5. Park in the driveway (as opposed to the garage).
6. Do not keep a garage door opener in your car or, at least, keep it out of view.
7. Tidy up anything a thief can use to access upper floor windows or doors, including ladders, patio furniture, a fence, tree branches, etc.

Additional Security Measures You Should Take

8. Never hide a spare key on your property and not under the doormat or atop the door frame.
9. Don't post your name on your mailbox or other outside signage.
10. Install a wide-angle peephole.
11. All non-traditional exterior doors (e.g., sliding doors) should have secondary locking devices.

12. Windows should have additional/secondary locks as well.
13. Remove the end from your garage door pull release handle.
14. Get a dog (especially the barking type).
15. Request a security inspection from local authorities (they might catch something you missed).
16. Join the neighborhood watch or start one.

First Impressions Really Do Matter

17. Trees and shrubs should be trimmed regularly especially next to windows and doors, though, all landscaping should be kept tidy to reduce potential hiding spots anywhere in your yard.
18. Install motion-sensing lights where possible, especially along the driveway and exterior doors.
19. Don't leave expensive toys (e.g., motorcycles, riding lawnmowers, etc.) in plain sight.
20. Fences are a double-edged sword as they both say, "stay out" but also offer additional secrecy for thieves, particularly the taller six-foot privacy fences.

Vacations and Holidays Are No Time to Relax

21. Ensure somebody trustworthy grabs your mail, newspapers, and even flyers left on your door.
22. Purchase a locking mailbox and/or put a hold on your mail.

23. Park a vehicle in the driveway or, better yet, ask your neighbor to park in your driveway.
24. Request an occasional drive by from local authorities.
25. Holiday garbage should be slowly and carefully disposed of.

The Three Most Effective Security Measures

1. Add a security alarm system. This is likely the most important action you can take, though, you must use it daily to be effective.
2. Add surveillance equipment, which is a close second; just ensure they're good quality, exterior cameras, that cover all entryways to your home. And it's best if they record for later review.
3. Prepare for your valuables to be stolen. Get insurance riders for expensive jewelry, antiques, electronics, and collectibles, to name a few. Beware if your firearms are stolen as you may be legally required to report theft. Last, take special care of all your handheld electronics since they include a goldmine of information on your identity. In fact, take steps now to protect yourself later should any electronics become lost or stolen, including:
   a. Record all serial numbers and secure them in a safe place (e.g., fire safe);
   b. Use "find my device" services to locate and even disable devices;

c. Password-protect all electronics to slow down would-be identity thieves;
d. Encrypt sensitive computer data using software such as VeraCrypt [Link 65];
e. Avoid accessing data on smart devices and/or move files to the Cloud;
f. Move sensitive data to an external USB drive and backup regularly;
g. Report theft to the authorities and insurance and change all passwords immediately.

Appendix B: List of Resources

- Link 1: https://rethinksurvival.com/books/home-security-checklist.php
- Link 2: https://rethinksurvival.com/books/home-security-book-offer.php
- Link 3: https://rethinksurvival.com/kindle-books/
- Link 4: https://rethinksurvival.com/kindle-books/id-theft-book/
- Link 5: https://www.crimereports.com/
- Link 6: http://www.eyewitnesssurveillance.com/americans-dont-lock-doors-survey/
- Link 7: https://nextdoor.com/
- Link 8: https://rethinksurvival.com/kindle-books/home-security-recommends/#keypadlock
- Link 9: https://www.youtube.com/watch?v=GwmcpukL7kE
- Link 10: https://rethinksurvival.com/kindle-books/home-security-recommends/#doorkit
- Link 11: https://rethinksurvival.com/kindle-books/home-security-recommends/#windowtint
- Link 12: https://rethinksurvival.com/kindle-books/home-security-recommends/#timer

- Link 13: https://rethinksurvival.com/kindle-books/home-security-recommends/#faketv
- Link 14: https://www.intelius.com/
- Link 15: https://www.gokeyless.com/blog/the-5-worst-places-to-hide-a-key/
- Link 16: https://rethinksurvival.com/kindle-books/home-security-recommends/#sprinklerkey
- Link 17: https://rethinksurvival.com/kindle-books/home-security-recommends/#lockbox
- Link 18: https://www.homedepot.com/c/installing_a_door_peep_hole_HT_PG_DW
- Link 19: https://rethinksurvival.com/kindle-books/home-security-recommends/#doorcamera
- Link 20: https://rethinksurvival.com/kindle-books/home-security-recommends/#slidingdoorbar
- Link 21: https://rethinksurvival.com/kindle-books/home-security-recommends/#pinlock
- Link 22: https://rethinksurvival.com/kindle-books/home-security-recommends/#swingbarlock
- Link 23: https://rethinksurvival.com/kindle-books/home-security-recommends/#securitybar

- Link 24: https://rethinksurvival.com/kindle-books/home-security-recommends/#securityfilm
- Link 25: https://rethinksurvival.com/kindle-books/home-security-recommends/#windowbar
- Link 26: https://www.youtube.com/watch?v=w7tr0N XRg5M
- Link 27: https://www.youtube.com/watch?v=kSO_H TBHLFI
- Link 28: https://cops.usdoj.gov/html/cd_rom/inaction 1/pubs/BurglaryofSingleFamilyHouses.pdf
- Link 29: https://rethinksurvival.com/kindle-books/home-security-recommends/#wirelesslights
- Link 30: https://holdmail.usps.com/holdmail/
- Link 31: http://chicago.cbslocal.com/2017/02/02/2-investigators-home-owner-thinks-post-office-tipped-off-burglars-she-was-gone/
- Link 32: https://www.vectorsecurity.com/blog/airef-study-highlights
- Link 33: https://simplisafe.com/
- Link 34: https://www.theguardian.com/business/2017

/aug/18/former-burglars-barking-dogs-cctv-best-deterrent
- Link 35: https://rethinksurvival.com/kindle-books/home-security-recommends/#lorexcameras
- Link 36: https://www.esurance.com/info/homeowners/hidden-valuables-in-your-home
- Link 37: http://lawcenter.giffords.org/gun-laws/policy-areas/gun-owner-responsibilities/reporting-lost-stolen-firearms/
- Link 38: https://myaccount.google.com/find-your-phone
- Link 39: https://www.absolutelojack.com/
- Link 40: http://www.gadgettrak.com/
- Link 41: http://www.lockittight.com/
- Link 42: https://www.preyproject.com/
- Link 43: https://www.pcworld.com/article/2835162/how-to-encrypt-sensitive-data-put-it-in-an-encrypted-container.html
- Link 44: https://rethinksurvival.com/kindle-books/secret-hides-book/
- Link 45: https://rethinksurvival.com/make-diy-diversion-safe-vegetable-can/
- Link 46: https://www.youtube.com/watch?v=oW9cYSuNRoU

- Link 47: https://rethinksurvival.com/kindle-books/secret-hides-recommends/#firesafe
- Link 48: https://www.youtube.com/watch?v=huwgI7b5in0
- Link 49: https://rethinksurvival.com/kindle-books/secret-hides-recommends/#wallsafe
- Link 50: https://rethinksurvival.com/kindle-books/id-theft-book/
- Link 51: https://www.youtube.com/watch?v=9f7hqglQZ7U
- Link 52: https://rethinksurvival.com/books/home-security-share.html
- Link 53: https://rethinksurvival.com/books/home-security-checklist.php
- Link 54: https://rethinksurvival.com/kindle-books/
- Link 55: https://rethinksurvival.com/kindle-books/bug-out-bag-book/
- Link 56: https://rethinksurvival.com/kindle-books/diy-survival-projects-book/
- Link 57: https://rethinksurvival.com/kindle-books/pet-safety-plan-book/
- Link 58: https://rethinksurvival.com/kindle-books/smartphone-survival-apps-book/
- Link 59: https://rethinksurvival.com/kindle-books/survival-foods-book/

- Link 60: https://rethinksurvival.com/kindle-books/secret-hides-book/
- Link 61: https://rethinksurvival.com/kindle-books/id-theft-book/
- Link 62: https://rethinksurvival.com/kindle-books/survival-uses-book/
- Link 63: https://rethinksurvival.com/books/new-survival-books.php
- Link 63b: https://rethinksurvival.com/kindle-books/id-theft-book/
- Link 64: https://rethinksurvival.com/books/home-security-review.php
- Link 65: https://veracrypt.codeplex.com/